SELF PUBLISH WORLDWIDE

How to Publish Your Book

Quickly, Affordably
And Make it Available Worldwide

By Ruth Barringham

Copyright © 2022 by Ruth Barringham

Published in Australia

Cheriton House Publishing

Updated 2024

The author is the copyright owner of this work, and no part may be reproduced by any process, nor may any other exclusive right be exercised without the permission of the Author.

This book is sold subject to the condition that it shall not, by way of trade or otherwise, be lent, re-sold, hired out, published electronically online or otherwise circulated without the Author's prior consent. All instances of copyright infringement will be dealt with to the full extent of the law.

ISBN: Paperback: 978-0-9803582-8-5

eBook: 978-0-9871151-9-5

Also by Ruth Barringham

How to Quit Smoking

How To Write An Article In 15 Minutes Or Less

Goodbye Writer's Block

7 Day eBook Writing and Publishing System

Living The Laptop Lifestyle

Mission Critical for Life

The 12 Month Writing Challenge

The Monthly Challenge Writing Series

Book 1 - Quick Cash Freelance Writing

Book 2 - Build A Lucrative Niche Website

Book 3 - Fast & Profitable Article Writing

Book 4 - The One Month Author

https://cheritonhousepublishing.com

Disclaimer:

The Author and Publisher have used their best efforts in preparing this book. The Author and Publisher make no representation or warranties with respect to the accuracy, applicability, fitness, or completeness of the contents of this book.

The Author is not a lawyer or an accountant and does not intend to render legal, accounting or other professional advice within this book. No guarantees of income, sales or results are promised. It is recommended that users of this book seek legal, accounting and other independent professional business advice before starting any business or acting upon any advice given herein.

The information contained in this book is strictly for information purposes. Therefore, if you wish to apply ideas contained in this book, you are taking full responsibility for your actions. Whilst we hope you find the contents of this book interesting and informative; the contents are for general information purposes only and do not constitute advice. We believe the contents to be true and accurate as at the date of writing but can give no assurances or warranty regarding the accuracy, currency, or applicability of any of the contents in relation to specific situations and particular circumstances.

This book is not intended to be a source for advice, and thus the reader should not rely on any information provided in this book as such. Readers should always seek the advice of an appropriately qualified person in the reader's home jurisdiction. The Author and Publisher of this book assume no responsibility for information contained in this book and disclaim all liability in respect of such information. In addition, none of the content of this book will form any part of any contract or constitute an offer of any kind.

Any links to third party websites are provided solely for the purpose of your convenience. Links made to websites are made at your own risk and the Author and Publisher accept no liability for any linked sites. When you access a website, please understand that it is independent from the Author and Publisher and the Author and Publisher have no control over the content of that website.

Further, a link contained in this book does not mean that the Author or Publisher endorses or accepts any responsibility for the content or the use of such website. The Author and Publisher do not give any representation regarding the quality, safety, suitability, or reliability of any of them or any of the material contained within them. Users must take their own precautions to ensure that what is selected for use is free of such items as viruses, worms, trojan horses and other items of a destructive nature.

All websites, products and services are mentioned, without warranty of any kind, either express or implied, including, but not limited to, the implied warranties of merchant ability and fitness for a particular purpose.

Some (but not many) of the links contained within this book are affiliate links to third party Companies, which means the publisher or author may receive a small payment/commission if any purchases are made or agreements signed with any of the third parties.

Table of Contents

Disclaimer: *5*
Table of Contents *7*

Introduction. 11
Self Publishing Means Freedom for Authors *11*
Freedom For Writers *13*
Self Publishing Made Millionaire Authors *13*
How Much Does Self Publishing Cost? *14*

Chapter 1. 17
Different Ways to Self Publish a Book *17*

Chapter 2. 20
Selling Fiction and Non-Fiction *20*
Writing Your Sales Page and Blurb *20*
Hypnotic Words *22*
Non-Fiction *25*
Fiction *25*

Chapter 3. 27
The Self-Publishing Process *27*
The Main Parts of a Book: *28*

Page Numbering 30
Copyright 30
Formatting 31
Formatting For a Printed Book 32
Publishing Jargon 36
ISBNs 44
Barcodes 46
Editions, Reprints and Imprints 47
Book Designers and Consultants 47
Chapter 4. 48
Print Books 48
Chapter 5. 58
eBook Publishing 58
Chapter 6. 62
Choosing Where to Publish 62
Chapter 7. 66
Libraries and Legals 66
Chapter 8. 72
Marketing 72
Book Reviews 73
Your Own Website 74
15 Ways to Market Your Book Online for Free 75
Chapter 9. 103
Quick start Self Publishing Guide 103

A Final Word...*106*

Introduction.

Hello and welcome to Self Publish worldwide – How to Publish Your Book Quickly, Affordably, And Make It Available Worldwide.

I previously updated this book in 2016. Back then self publishing was a lot different to what it is now. Thankfully it's changed for the better and now it's so easy to write and publish books and eBooks. In fact, with computers and online publishing, it's possible to write and publish a book every week, and I know authors who've done this. Many still do.

All it takes is the consistency to sit and write every day, plus a simple self publishing system, which is what we're going to look at.

Self Publishing Means Freedom for Authors

Not too long ago, it was difficult to become a published author because you had to write a book and try to get a publishing company interested in publishing it.

Back then, there were only printed books (no electronic books), and they were produced in huge print runs of tens of thousands of copies at a time, that were then trucked to bookstores and libraries, so only publishing companies had the money and expertise to do this.

And it was estimated that only one in fifty thousand manuscripts submitted to publishers were accepted, so most writers could only dream of working as full-time authors.

What truly revolutionized self publishing was the advent of print-on-demand (POD). In 1997, Lightning Source, one of the largest POD companies, was founded.

Previously, self published authors had to bear the costs of printing up-front, without knowing how many copies (if any) of their books would sell.

POD was a freeing for indie authors because now books could be Printed on Demand. This freed up authors to write because they were able to publish all their own books and only print one copy when it was ordered, and it was mailed directly to the customer.

At the time, many people poo-pooed the idea of publishing this way and warned that allowing authors to publish their own books would lead to a flood of low-quality writing hitting the bookstore shelves. They said that the reading public would never embrace it.

But they did.

What it led to, was online bookstores appearing all over the internet because now they didn't need to stock books anymore. Using Print on Demand they could just order a book whenever a customer made a purchase.

Then self publishing became even more exciting when eBooks and eBook reading apps and devices came along.

This completely revolutionized self publishing because now customers could not only buy a book, but they could also read it instantly.

Again, the poo-pooers said it would never work because readers want physical books in their hands, not words to read on a screen. And once again they were wrong.

eReaders meant that people could have all their books on one small device and take them anywhere.

eBooks changed the publishing industry so much that many publishing companies and book distribution companies went out of business.

Freedom For Writers

Finally, authors were free to write and publish as many books as they wanted. Gone was the need to write, print, submit manuscripts to publishing companies, and employ expensive editors to ensure their work was "worthy" of publication.

Self publishing was popular with authors, not just because of the freedom to write and publish all their books, but because of the ease and speed that it could be done, and because they were selling their own books, they could keep all the profit, which from eBook sales, was 100%.

Publishing companies only paid low royalties to authors, which was usually less than 10% of the sale price of the book. Self publishing companies charge a fee for each book sold and let authors keep the rest.

Readers have also benefited from self published authors because they now have access to millions more books, and with eReaders they can travel the world and take their whole library of books with them.

Self Publishing Made Millionaire Authors

Many authors have become millionaires through publishing their own books; and the list just keeps growing.

Amanda Hocking embraced self publishing early by publishing only a small number of her novels as eBooks for the Amazon Kindle, and as sales increased, she soon found herself earning half a million dollars a month.

John Locke also embraced eBook publishing early. He'd already written several novels and as soon as he heard about Kindle eBook publishing he published all his novels this way. His success is described in detail in his first non-fiction book "How I Sold 1 Million eBooks in 5 months."

And there have been many others enjoying millionaire status from self-publishing, including HP Malloy, Lee Goldberg, and JA Konrath, just to name a few.

But you don't have to publish for the Kindle to be successful in self-publishing. There are people like Jim Edwards and Dr Joe Vitale who were ridiculously successful selling eBooks from their own websites.

There are now far more self-published authors than those with traditional publishing contracts.

And Indie authors produce more book titles on a mass scale than any publishing company has ever done.

How Much Does Self Publishing Cost?

It used to be the cost of printing thousands of books at once (and the lack of storage space) that stopped authors from publishing their own work. But now, not only is it really cheap to self publish a book, but it can also be done for free with no upfront costs.

For instance, you can publish your book as a POD print book and an eBook using Amazon's Kindle Publishing platform. Or use a company like Ingram Sparks. Both these companies let you publish your book for free, and charge a small fee for each book sold, plus printing costs.

On the other hand, if you have money to spare you could pay a vanity publishing company to do all the publishing work for you.

Or you could not pay anyone and sell your own eBooks from your own blog or website. It is possible to produce your own eBooks using software on your own computer. My Mac Book allows me to save documents as epub files which can be read on most eReader apps and devices. Or I can use free software to save files as PDF documents that can be read on just about any device.

The choice is yours, and it may depend on what you're publishing and who your target audience is.

And we'll look at all of that soon. For now just enjoy the fact that self-publishing is simple and fast and can be done in minutes.

Chapter 1.

Different Ways to Self Publish a Book

Sometimes, when you start looking into self-publishing, it's written in such jargon that the more you read, the more confused you become.

So what I'm going to do is try and cut through all the technical stuff and all the publishing jargon to help you understand the different publishing opportunities open to you and how to use them.

4 Different Ways to Publish a Book

There are 4 ways to publish a book:

- Traditional Publishing
- Print Publishing
- eBook Publishing
- Vanity Publishing

Traditional Publishing

Traditional publishing is so called because traditionally it was the only way to get a book published.

It means pitching your manuscript to a literary agent or publishing company to try and encourage them to publish your book for you.

Sadly, because only about one in fifty thousand pitches are successful, and if it's accepted, it will probably be 18 months to 2 years before it's been through the editing and proofing process and is published. And authors only earn a small royalty from each sale.

Authors also have to market their books themselves, so once the book is published, the author has to do everything they can to increase sales which usually includes doing a book-signing tour.

Publishing companies expect large sales and may remove a book from their catalogue if it sells less than 40,000 copies a year. Publishing companies put a lot of time and money into publishing a book and do print runs of thousands of copies at a time, so they expect a high return.

This is why they are extremely careful about which books they choose to publish. If they get it wrong it can be extremely costly for them.

Vanity Publishing

This works in much the same way as traditional publishing except that the author pays to have their book published and there are no huge print runs.

Vanity publishing companies usually offer a range of services so that authors can pick and choose the publishing package they want depending on how much they want to pay. Publishing your book this way usually costs from a few hundred dollars to a few thousand.

The biggest problem with paying to have your book published is that it can take a long time before you break even. Plus you don't get paid 100% for every sale. The company only pays you a royalty from sales of around 25% to 40%.

There are plenty of authors who are quite willing to use a vanity publishing company because it saves them all the work involved with:

- Cover design
- Book registration
- Dealing with printing companies
- Editing
- Formatting
- And more

But beware. I've heard many horror stories from authors who didn't read the fine print of their publishing contract, and when they try and cancel, the company won't release the formatted book files, or the book cover design, and still keep the book registered to their company.

So, if you do want to try the vanity publishing route, choose a reputable company and read the online reviews from both satisfied and dissatisfied customers.

But this book isn't about using publishing companies. It's about the freedom and control to publish all your own books and sell them worldwide, hopefully selling thousands of copies every month.

The more books you write, the more books you can sell, and it can all be done from your own computer.

And once you've been through the self-publishing process once, it's so easy to do it again, and you have your accounts and systems already set up.

And even if you do decide to go the traditional or vanity publishing route, it will still be invaluable for you to read the rest of this book so that you'll understand the whole publishing process and all the jargon they'll throw at you.

Now, let's get going and look at the first thing you need to do.

Chapter 2.

Selling Fiction and Non-Fiction

Now I don't know if you've written a fiction book or non-fiction, or if you want to write both.

It doesn't really matter what your book is about because the publishing process is the same. The only difference is how you try and sell it.

This is the first step and it's so important that it can make or break your publishing success.

You must do it first and get it absolutely right before you can begin the physical process of publishing your book.

Writing Your Sales Page and Blurb

Believe it or not, writing great sales copy is more important than writing a great book. You can sell a mediocre book with great sales copy, but you can't sell a great book with mediocre sales copy.

There are two types of sales copy that you need to write.

- The sales page
- The back cover blurb

Of course, if you're only planning to publish eBooks, then you won't have a back cover to put the blurb on. But you will need sales page copy whether it's for a page on your own website, or blog, or an online bookstore sales page.

Sometimes it's a good idea to write your sales copy first, before you even begin to write your book.

Why?

Because when you write your sales page you come up with ideas about why your book is so great. It's like doing a brain-storming session and it can help you come up with great ideas for content that should be in your book.

Even if you're writing fiction you can write about how powerful your story is or the morals it contains, and all the emotions it will evoke.

If your book is already written it's still easy to write powerful sales copy for it, and it won't be too late to add any great ideas.

And as you write your sales copy you WILL come up with great ideas about the benefits of reading your book. By the time you've finished writing it, your sales copy will be so irresistible that readers will be itching to grab a copy of your book, and that's why you should always provide an instantly downloadable eBook copy.

The most important part of a sales page is the words. Fancy images and graphics don't make the sales. It's the words.

Also keep search engines in mind and make sure you use the correct keywords so that anyone searching for the topic or story you've written your book about will find it in the top 10 results. (More on this later).

Don't come across as salesy, even though you're trying to make a sale.

Your writing should be professional, but it also needs to sound personal, as though you're talking to a friend and telling them how great your book is and how it will benefit them, as though you wrote your book especially for them.

If your book is non-fiction, you can identify a problem they're having and show them how your book can help them.

Use phrases like:

- Imagine if
- You'll discover
- Wouldn't it be wonderful if
- The secret to

To help you even more, below is a list of words that are regarded as 'Hypnotic' and can be used to smoothly draw your readers into your sales copy.

Hypnotic Words

Achieve

Boost

Complete

Crammed

Delivered

Easy

Enjoy

Exciting

Explode

Floodgates

Foothold

Fortune

Fundamentals

Gross

Growth

Immediately

Incredible

Now

Obsession

Opportunities

Outstanding

Own

Potential

Power

Powerful

Practical

Professional

Profit From

Proven

Quickly

Rare

Remarkable

Results

Reveals

Rewards

Save

Secrets

Simplistic

Skill

Solution

Successful

Superior

Sure-fire

Surprising

Uncover

Unique

Unlimited

Unparalleled

Valuable

Vital

Want

Wealth

Wonderful

Yes

You

You're

To help make writing sales copy easy, you can use a question-and-answer session to work out all the benefits of your book for the reader. Come up with questions that they may ask about your book.

Go through the questions one at a time. Allow your mind to think freely and write down everything that comes to you, no matter how overwhelming or insignificant it seems.

Don't miss out any details.

Write down your answers as fully and completely as possible.

By the time you're finished answering all the questions, you should have several pages of writing in front of you.

Non-Fiction

What are your book's features? (make a list)

How will each one benefit the reader? (can be more than one benefit)

What problems will your book solve?

What benefit is the most important?

How is your book different?

What makes it better than all other similar books?

Fiction

What is your book about? (2-3 sentences)

What is the story? (full description)

How does it end? (happy twist, shocking, terrifying, touching)

What is the most important part of the story?

How is your book different to all the other similar books?

How will it leave the reader feeling?

You also need to understand your reader:
- Who will buy your book?
- What motivates them?
- What are their concerns about your book?
- Who are you NOT aiming your book at?

When you've finished and read through what you've written, you'll probably find that you've written most of your sales copy without even realizing it.

When you write your back page blurb for the printed versions of your book it will be a simple matter of choosing the most important and hypnotic parts of your sales page copy.

Once your sales copy is finished and you've chosen a curiosity invoking headline, you can publish it on your website or blog. Even though your book isn't published yet, it doesn't hurt to start your marketing machine going by publishing your sales page and adding "coming soon" or something similar.

You can also use your sales copy as your book description for the online bookstores.

Having your sales copy ready ahead of time is important because you don't want to start the publishing process and find that when you get to the part where you're asked to upload your book description, you have to stop and start writing it from scratch.

And now with all the writing out of the way, it's time to start publishing.

Chapter 3.

The Self-Publishing Process

In this chapter we're going to look at the overall self-publishing process, including different parts of a book, how to format it, and "jargon" words you need to know.

As we go through it all (and I'll be as brief and succinct as I can) it may seem a little daunting. But don't worry. Things always do if you've never tried them before.

And at the end of this book I've included a Quick Start Guide that lists each thing you need to do and in what order. So let's start looking at the self-publishing process.

Parts of a Book

As well as the content of your book, there are other pages to include. Most are optional but one of them, the publishing page is a must, as I'll explain later.

For now, before you can publish your book, it needs to contain all the necessary pages so it's helpful to understand the different parts of the book, which will also assist you when dealing with publishing and printing companies, if you need them.

Leaves and Pages

Leaves are the cut sheets of paper that make up a book and are usually printed on both sides. The front of the leaf (on the right side of an open book) is called the recto. The other side (on the left-hand side of an open book) is called the verso.

Go through the following list and make sure that your book has all the necessary pages added to it.

The Main Parts of a Book:

Prelims

The preliminary pages are the first few pages before the main content of your book begins.

Text

The text is the main body of your book, and the first page is always on the recto (the right-hand page of an open book).

End Matter

This is the last few pages of a book which can include the index, glossary, appendices, notes, bibliography, contributors, etc.

Pages in the Prelims

The first page of a book (recto) usually only has your book's title. This title page can also include the subtitle, author or publisher's name.

Publishing Information Page

This page contains the publisher's name and address, date of publication, edition number, ISBN, copyright information, author's assertion of rights, disclaimer that all rights are reserved, name of printer and, often, the typeface your book is set in. This page is usually printed on a verso page.

Dedication

Some authors like to include this page to dedicate a book to someone who has helped or influenced them.

Epigraph

This is not essential and is a suitable quotation from another piece of literature.

Acknowledgements

A page for a "thank you" speech.

Disclaimer

This is a statement that is intended as a safeguard from legal action arising from anyone using the information contained in the book. A disclaimer isn't always necessary, depending on the content of your book.

Table of Contents

A list of contents within the book.

List of Illustrations

A list of illustrations within the book.

Foreword

A further set of acknowledgements.

Preface

An introduction to a book written by the author of the book.

Introduction

An introduction to the main part of your book.

Page Numbering

Page numbering includes the prelims although they don't usually have to be printed on them. The Introduction and Preface pages are usually numbered separately in Roman Numerals. The main page numbers are usually placed at the centre at the top of the page or centre at the bottom.

Ensure that the first page of the book's main content always begins on a recto (right-hand) page and that the first line of each chapter is never indented.

These pages and layout of your book aren't compulsory but are universally understood by all readers and so are always expected. To set out your book any differently would not only confuse the reader, but it would look amateurish.

Copyright

For your own protection you should find a copyright agency to register your book with before you publish it (or preferably as soon as you finish writing it). This will help to protect you if anyone accuses you of plagiarism or any other kind of copyright infringement.

Once your book is registered with a copyright agency (which can be done online in only a few minutes) they can also handle any queries from anyone who wants to legally copy part of your work and they can also handle fees and payments on your behalf.

Some of the following agencies might be of use:

https://www.cla.co.uk/

https://www.copyright.com.au/

https://www.copyright.com/

Formatting

When it comes to having your manuscript converted to a digital file ready for POD publishing or eBook publishing, the best and easiest way to do it is to keep your formatting basic.

It's best to format it as you write it, using 'styles' to set up titles, headings, font, and paragraphs, etc. If you didn't, then you need to do it before you publish your book.

One of the things I find handy is to set up the styles for one book and save it as a template for subsequent books too.

Most self-publishing companies want you to upload a word document (doc.x) or a text document (rtf), so if you use Pages for Mac like I do you'll need to convert (export) it to another file type before you can publish it. Never try and upload a PDF file. These have rigid formatting which don't convert well to digital formats (epub, .mobi, etc.) and most websites won't allow you to upload PDF files.

For the print version of your book, you'll need to use Mirror Margins, which are the margins next to the centre of your pages.

Books usually have justified lines.

Don't use very large or very small fonts.

Anything less than 12pt is too hard to read.

It's recommended to use 12pt size for the body text and 14pt to 18pt for chapter titles.

For your eBook version, don't have page numbers in your Table of Contents because eReaders allow viewers to change the page layout and font size so the page numbers don't matter. Just make sure you put a hard page break at the end of each chapter.

Also for eBooks, make sure your images are no more than 300px high. Don't resize them on the page. Remove them, resize them, then copy and paste them back in.

When it comes to converting files for publication, you'll find that every company has different ideas of exactly how they want your file. Basic is still the best and safest way to go to begin with. But once you find a website (company) you want to work with, read their formatting guide, often called a Style Guide, and make any necessary adjustments if needed.

It's easy to format your manuscript using the word processing software on your own computer, and no matter who you choose to publish your book, they won't be asking for anything else.

Formatting For a Printed Book

Page Sizes

Firstly you'll need to change your page size and probably your font and margins too.

First, lay out your manuscript on A5 size pages (go to the File menu and click on "page setup" and choose your page size) then adjust the margins so that your text will fit comfortably on the page of the eventual trimmed size of your printed book. Allow a margin of at least 2cm on the right margin and 2.5 on the left margin. Also adjust your top and bottom margins to 2cm.

It is also important that you click on "Mirror Margins" in your Page Setup. This sets your page layout for left and right pages that "mirror" each other, just like in an open book.

If you're using Pages for Mac, click on the "inspector" link in the menu bar, then "document inspector" in the top of the window that opens (it's a little image of a blank page) and then click on "facing pages."

If you're at all unsure of how your finished page should look, just take a few similar books from your own bookshelves and see how they are laid out.

Font Size

Word's default font size is 10 point but this is too small to comfortably read in paperback. Most paperbacks are best to read with a minimum of 40 characters per line and maximum of 70. 40 is the most comfortable small font size for most readers, which is 12 point. Note: there are 72 points to 1 inch.

Text in printed books is always justified.

Font Face

Word's default font face, or more correctly, typeface, is Times New Roman. This typeface is so called because it was designed to be the best typeface for the narrow columns of print in the Times Newspaper and so was never intended to be used in books.

Another typeface of greater width would be more suitable. Try using Palatino or Georgia or Arial.

Line Spacing

Word's standard line spacing is "single", "1.5" or "double". A more preferred line spacing should be set to an exact point measurement that is 2 to 4 points larger than your font size. For example, if your font size is 12 point, go into the Format menu and choose paragraph. For line spacing select "at least" or "exactly" and then choose 14 to 16 point (or set line spacing to 1.2, 1.3 or 1.4).

Characters

Make sure you use "typographic" characters and not "typewriter" characters. For instance, use "smart quotes" instead of "straight quotes" and don't use single hyphens (-) or double hyphens (--) instead of a dash (–) or "em dash" as it's correctly called.

To use correct characters go to the Insert menu and choose "symbol" to find the right typographic character. Alternatively, go into the Tools menu, choose "Auto Correct" and "Auto Format" and "Auto Format as you Type". Using this option changes characters as you type.

Remember to also use "justified" for your page layout.

Styles

Word has a Style feature that allows you to apply different styles and attributes to selected text. The style will then continue to change automatically to all text governed by that style.

For instance, if you want all your headings to be size 16 font and underlined and all your subheadings to be size 12 font and bold, you can set up a style to do this for you automatically. It's easy to set up, and using styles can save you an enormous amount of time while writing your book and it also ensures consistency. You can also store styles in a template to use again in a future book.

You can find Styles under the Format menu in Windows and under View menu in Pages for Mac.

Styles can also assist you when you want to insert an automatic Table of Contents. You can find this under the Insert menu.

Automatic Kerning

Kerning means moving individual letters closer or further apart to make the text appear more even.

Word does have automatic kerning which can be turned on in the Format menu and choosing "character spacing". This is simply called character spacing in Pages for Mac and can be found under the Inspector menu and choosing Text Inspector (it looks like a big "T" at the top of the Inspector window).

Kerning doesn't usually improve justified blocks of text, but it works well when used on single lines of text such as titles and headings.

Page Breaks

Word can insert page breaks so that even if you go back and add more text the page will still end exactly where you inserted the page break. This is important when using chapters.

Go to the Insert menu and choose "insert break" and then click "page break". Make sure your curser is already positioned where you want the page break.

You can also use the "line break" option to ensure text always begins on a new line. On the view menu, choose "show all" to see where these breaks have been placed. This will also show character spacing.

Windows and Orphans

Always avoid Windows and Orphans.

An orphan is the first line of a paragraph that appears at the bottom of a page by itself or has a heading above it, and continues on the next page.

A window is the opposite of this and is the last line of a paragraph that appears at the top of a page by itself.

Word usually avoids windows and orphans by default. But if it doesn't, go into the Format menu, click on "paragraph" and then choose "line and page breaks" and turn it on there.

Following all the suggestions here will produce work that's about 90% as accurate as using the other software packages.

And if you use Pages on your Mac computer, under the Format menu you find "Export...". You can use this feature to save your Pages document as a plain text document, a Word document, a Rich Text document, a PDF document (with password security settings) or an ePub file (more on ePub files later). This makes creating an eBook so much easier with no other software required.

Publishing Jargon

Publishing companies and printing companies regularly use words that are considered "jargon" to those not used to dealing with them. In order to understand these terms better, here is a Jargon-Busting list of words that you will most likely come across while publishing a book:

Artwork

Pictures, drawings, sketches or any other type of illustration (but not a photograph) that is in its finished form and ready to go to the printer.

Barcode

Computer coded information represented by a row of black and white lines, and is usually found on the back of books. Barcodes are used by stores to record and order all stock.

Bibliography

A list of where information was sourced from in the writing of the book. The bibliography is usually found in the final pages of a book.

Binding

The method used for holding the pages and cover together of a book.

Bleed

The extra colours around the edge of a book cover so that it runs off the cut edge and shows no blank (white) spaces.

Blurb

A brief description of the contents of a book and is usually found on the back cover of a paperback book or the inside flap of a hardback book.

Body Type

The typeface, or font, used for the majority of the text. The headings and subheadings will probably be of a different typeface.

Book Designers (Book Consultants)

People who oversee the whole production process of a book from typed manuscript to printed book. They may even provide a cover design as part of their service.

Camera Ready Copy (CRC)

Hard copy of the pages of a book laid out ready for printing that are then photographed as the first part of the printing process.

Cartridge paper

Printing paper with a matt finish.

Case Binding

The hard cover of a book.

Cloth Binding

A hardback book with a cloth cover.

Colophon

A publisher's logo.

Commission

The amount of money usually paid to distributors and is normally a percentage of the cover price.

Computer to Plate (CTP)

When the text is taken straight from an electronic file to the printer, negating the need for CRC processing.

Copy

The text of a manuscript is often referred to as copy.

Copy Fitting

Estimating the amount of space or pages that the text will fill, by counting the average number of characters and spaces per line and dividing the number of words in the text by the result.

Desktop Publishing

Producing a book as CRC by using a computer, the appropriate desktop publishing software and a laser printer.

Display Type

Typeface, or font, that is different from the main body of the text, such as headings or sub headings.

Dummy

A sample book, or set of pages, made to give an idea of how the finished book will look.

Edition

The original production of a book. Any further editions have extensive changes such as hard back to paper back or have the text significantly changed, such as a book that has been updated. Each edition requires a different ISBN.

Embossing

Raised images or text on the cover of a book. Can be used on paperback covers or case bound book jackets.

End Matter

Pages of information at the end of a book which can include appendices, bibliography, glossary, author information or an index.

EPublishing

Producing and selling electronic downloadable books on the internet.

Flopped

An image that has been printed the wrong way round (reversed).

Folio

The number of each page in a book.

Glossary

A list of words used in the book, with a short explanation of their meaning.

Gutter

The margin on the edge of a book where the spine will be. The Gutter will need to be wider than the other 3 margins around the page to accommodate this.

Half Tone

Also known as continuous tone. An image made of dots that has graduations of tone from light to dark. Can be a photograph or artwork.

Illustration

Any non-text based addition to a book.

Imposition

The arrangement of pages on large sheets that ensure that when folded, they fall in the correct order.

Lamination

A thin, transparent film of plastic or varnish that is applied as protection to a cover or jacket.

Limp Binding

The binding of a book which is much the same as the binding of a hard back book, i.e., the sections are sewn at the spine and end papers attached on the spine, front and back, but there are no boards in the covers, thus making the book "limp".

Line Artwork

Illustrations that are made up of only black and white lines or solid black areas.

Manuscript

An author's final text of a book. Often abbreviated as MS or MSS.

Margin

The white spaces at the edges of every page of a book. Usually the bottom margin and the one near the spine (the gutter) are wider than the other two.

Mark-up

Instructions of how the manuscript will be formatted such as font, headings, type size. This is usually already encoded into digital copies of the manuscript.

Off Set Printing

Also known as Off Set Lithography. A common printing process where the pages are transposed onto metal plates which are then inked and pressed onto paper.

Overrun

Extra copies of a book that are printed for the publisher to use for publicity.

Page Proof

Completed pages showing that the text, headings and illustrations are placed correctly. Page proofs are used to check that everything is correct so that amendments can be made if necessary. Publishers usually express how many page proofs are required before printing can go ahead.

Perfect Binding

A flat, glued spine that is usually found on a paperback book.

PostScript

A software program that instructs devices such as printers, as to how to layout a page and keep correct formatting.

Prelims

The first few pages of a book before the main text begins, and usually consists of title page, table of contents, copyright page and other pages as well.

Pre-press

The entire printer processes required before the actual printing of a book takes place.

Print Consultant

A specialist who commissions the correct binding and printing methods used to produce a finished book or other printed material.

Print Run

Number of copies of a publication that are printed.

Recto

The right-hand page of an open book.

Register

Check to ensure that all printed pages are exactly in the correct relation to each other when still on the same sheet. A 4-colour page will have to have each layer of colour in the correct position to ensure that the next layer of colour will be placed correctly. Markers will be used on each sheet to ensure correct colour placement.

Reprint

A new printing of a book with little or no alterations.

Resolution

The number of pixels, or dots, per inch that make up an image. Usually the more pixels or dots, the better the image quality. Printers usually ask for an image of 300-600dpi.

Reverse Out

To change a coloured (or black) image on a white background, to a white image on a coloured (or black) background.

Runover

Text that runs over from one line into another or from one page onto another.

Saddle Stitching

Folds of a booklet held together with wire staples.

Screen

A mesh screen that changes a continuous tone image into a half tone image by the use of small dots.

Sections

Large sheets of paper that the pages are printed on and then folded to form a section of a book.

Slipcase

A box which a set of books can be housed in that still shows the spines.

Spot Colour

An extra single colour used to provide emphasis to a particular text or illustration.

Spread

Two facing pages of an open book or magazine.

TIFF

Tagged Image File Format. A digital file that can include a scanned line drawing.

Title

Another name for a book.

Trim marks

Marks that show the actual size of the finished book.

Typestyle

The name of the font used, such as Times New Roman, Arial or Verdana. Also includes other variations such as bold or italic and the size.

Unit Cost

The total cost of producing each individual copy of a book.

Verso

The left-hand page of an open book.

Windows and Orphans

A window is a single word or single line of text at the top of a page that has run-on from a paragraph on the previous page. An orphan is a single word or line of text at the bottom of a page that continues on the next page. Both are to be avoided.

ISBNs

An International Standard Book Number is usually referred to as an ISBN.

It's a unique 13-digit number assigned to each book. ISBNs aren't compulsory, but they do make it simple to identify your book. It's the way that bookstores and online stores order your book, and most of them won't stock your book or sell it without one.

So precise are ISBNs to find an exact copy of a book, that each edition and each binding of your book must have a different ISBN.

For instance, if you publish a book as a hardcover and a paperback and as an eBook, you'll need a separate ISBN for each one.

The easiest way to obtain an ISBN is through a company called R R Bowker. They can be found in the US, the UK and Australia. You can buy ISBNs online at:

https://www.bowker.com.

https://www.myidentifiers.com.au/

R R Bowker isn't the only place you can buy ISBNs from, but you need to be aware that R R Bowker is the exclusive source of ISBNs. There are many unauthorized resellers of ISBNs and they need to be avoided if at all possible. These people buy ISBNs and resell them for a higher price. So use R R Bowker if you live in the US, UK or Australia, or use an official ISBN agency in your own country.

You can find a whole list of International ISBN agencies and an instantly downloadable ISBN manual at

https://www.isbn-international.org/agencies.html.

You can buy just one ISBN (in most countries), or a block of 10, 100, 1,000, etc. If you're planning to write several books or you want to publish your book in different formats, then you really need to purchase a block of 10 or more.

Once you've bought your block of ISBNs you don't need to assign them to a book straight away. You can keep them for your next books so that your ISBNs are numerical. But make sure they send you all of your numbers at once otherwise they won't be numerical.

Bowker also runs another website at https://www.myidentifiers.com. This is another place where you can list your books once you have your ISBNs. This site uses your same login information as the Bowker main sites. On this site you can even upload a PDF of your book so that Bowker can find keywords from the content to help let customers find your book. This site even lists your ISBNs before you have assigned them.

There is a plethora of information on the internet and in other books as to where you should list your book to let it be known globally that it is available. But Bowker is by far the most important so if you don't list it anywhere else, make sure you list it here.

Barcodes

Book cover barcodes should be added to the bottom of the back cover of a book. It should contain the same numbers as your ISBN which should be printed above it.

Retail stores, and some online bookstores, won't accept a book without a barcode if it's a printed book they want to physically stock.

If you've printed copies of your book without a barcode, you can purchase barcode stickers from most printing companies.

Some people will try and tell you that you need to include an EAN (European Article Number) on your barcode, but it really isn't necessary.

All manufactured retail goods are issued with an EAN (European Article Number). This is a 13-digit number just like an ISBN, so with books you only need the ISBN and not an EAN. In Japan, they use a JAN (Japanese Article Number), but again, your ISBN can be used instead of this.

Some years ago all retail products were given a UPC (Universal Product Code) number. UPCs were eventually replaced with EANs.

EAN, ISBN, UPC and JAN are all collectively called Global Trade Item Numbers.

N.B. A point worth mentioning here is that it would be wise to go online and search to see if anyone else has the same book title as the one you want to use.

Even with the use of ISBNs and Barcodes, it can still be confusing if two books have exactly the same title. If someone else is using your preferred title, perhaps you could change yours by adding a different subtitle.

Editions, Reprints and Imprints

An Edition is a reprint of a book that includes large revisions and updates. Each edition requires a new ISBN.

A Reprint simply means a new print run of the same book with no changes or only minor changes so the book stays essentially the same.

An Imprint (or impression, as it's sometimes called) is a book that is marketed as different "imprints" within a publishing company. For instance, if a publisher brought out a romantic horror novel, it would publish it through its horror division (imprint) AND its romance division to try and reach a wider audience.

Book Designers and Consultants

If you don't like the thought of getting your manuscript ready for publishing yourself, you could hire a book designer, or book consultant as they're sometimes called.

They take your book all the way from finished manuscript right through to the printing and publishing process.

They do everything for you that a vanity publishing company would do, except publish it.

They will do everything else however, including formatting the interior of your book, providing a copyright page, etc. and produce a book cover.

Chapter 4.

Print Books

The Printing Process

When you self-publish a book it's helpful if you understand a little about the printing process. So this chapter will describe what happens to your book when it arrives at the printing company.

Printing companies usually speak of a book in 2 halves:

The book cover (front, spine and back)

The book block (inner pages)

Your book cover and your book block are usually saved as two separate files and are sent to the printer electronically.

Paper

Paper comes in different "weights" and these are measured in grams per square metre or "gsm".

Normal photocopy paper is 80gsm. The thicker or denser, the paper, the heavier its weight. Most books are produced on 70 to 90gsm paper.

If your book contains colour illustrations or photographs, the paper will need to be at least 100gsm to prevent the images from showing through on the other side of the page. Photographs will also need to be on glossy, coated paper.

Some digital printing companies can print photographs on normal paper along with all the other pages, but they won't be as glossy as using photo paper although they still look good.

When self-publishing, bear in mind that the weight of the paper will affect the weight and thickness of the finished book so using lighter paper will reduce transport, distribution and postage and storage costs.

Printers refer to paper as "stock".

Stock comes in certain standard sizes:

A1:	594 x 841mm
A2:	420 x 594mm
A3:	297 x 420mm
A4:	210 x 297mm
A5:	148 x 210mm
A6:	105 x 148mm
A7:	74 x 105mm

There are also several pre-metric sizes:

Crown 8VO:	123 x 186mm
Large Crown 8VO:	129 x 198mm
Demy: 8VO:	138 x 216mm
Royal 8VO:	156 x 234mm

Printers can cut books to any size requested but using non-standard sizes can mean a lot of paper wasted and a lot higher cost. Some printers (and publishers) use a small font size to use less paper. But readers don't like this and when deciding on which book to buy may simply choose the one that's easier to read.

Illustrations

There are 4 different types of book illustrations:

Line drawings

Photographs

Screen shots (i.e. from a computer)

Original artwork

The easiest to scan and reproduce are line drawings, which are exactly as their name suggests. They are drawings made from lines and are also known as "sketches".

But all the different types of illustrations can be scanned into a computer and then manipulated onscreen to produce the desired result. Photographs can also be resized and retouched to really enhance them.

Photographs are known as continuous tone art and will need to be screened. Screening is a process that makes the photographs printable by breaking them up into dots.

Images screened this way are known as half tones.

Most printing companies prefer images to be at least 300dpi (dots per inch) to ensure good reproductive quality.

Your book cover needs to be the exact size for the final book's "trimmed size", that is, the eventual size your book will be cut to, and also have about 1mm to 2mm of "bleed". This means extra background colour around the edges so that no white paper will show.

Printing for the cover is done in 4 colours – cyan, magenta, yellow and black (CMYB).

Books are printed on large sheets of paper in multiples of 4, 8, 16, 32 or 64 pages. Once printed, the sheets are folded short end to short end and then long side to long side. As you can imagine, the printed pages are in quite different places when the sheets are still unfolded, and some will even have to be printed upside down so that they are positioned correctly in the final folded and trimmed book block.

Once the sheets are folded, they are called "sections" and are then cut to size by guillotine.

Hardback books, or "case bound" books, are cased in a hard cover. The folded sheets of paper (sections) are trimmed only at the top to remove the folds and then the sections are stitched on the remaining fold. All the section folds are then attached to a backing strip which is then attached to the board covers by sheets called "end papers" which can be a different colour or have a printed design.

Hard back books are usually given a paper jacket – or "dust jacket". This has the extra space on the wrap-around for promotional material and author biographies.

Some hard back books have boards covered in cloth and so are called "cloth bound".

Paperbacks have all the folds in the sections cut off. The sections are then laid together and glued into the spine of your book. This is called Perfect Binding and is the cheapest way of producing a book.

Not too many years ago, paperback books were well-known for falling apart at the spine so the reader ended up with pages coming loose throughout the book.

These days, modern adhesives have made paperback books more robust although books with very wide spines can still cause problems.

It's always a good idea to order a proof copy of your printed book to check that the cover and spine are ok and that all the pages are printed in the right order.

Creating a Book Cover

Some printing companies will do this for you, or they will employ another company to do it on their behalf.

Alternatively, you can surf the internet for book cover designers. These people are usually incredibly creative at what they do, but they can charge from several hundred dollars to several thousand.

Book cover designers will usually provide all photos and images for you if you don't have your own. They can usually supply a small logo for the spine too.

If you want a professional book cover, do a search online for book cover designers. They are usually extremely creative at what they do, but they can be expensive. However they will provide all photos or artwork if you don't have your own.

Another option is to download book cover design software.

Most self-publishing companies also provide free book cover templates as part of the service, so all you have to do is provide the photo or artwork for the front cover.

Sometimes I use my own computer to design a front cover using the basic word processing software (Pages for Mac). Then I either save it as an image or take a screenshot of it. Then I match the background colour to the spine and back cover.

And although I've never tried it, there are plenty of free tutorials online showing how to make print book covers using GIMP, the free image editing software.

If you're planning on publishing many books, and I hope you are, having your own book cover software would be a good investment.

I use Adobe In-Design. It's not cheap but it's well worth it.

But many authors have successfully published all their books using nothing more than the free book cover software provided by their self-publishing company and using free, online images, or AI.

Book Wholesalers and Distributors

I would assume that the way you want to self-publish your book is by using an online self-publishing company and sell your printed books via POD, as previously discussed.

If you prefer to sell your printed books yourself then the following information will be useful. If you are planning on using POD, then the following information is still useful for showing you how print distribution works.

Once your book is printed and your publication day is set, what you need to do next is find a company to distribute your book to bookstores.

There are 3 different types of company that will do this for you:

- Wholesalers
- Distributors
- Jobbers

Wholesalers buy books at a discount and sell them on to retail stores. But this is all they do. They don't actively go out and promote books or visit retail stores to take orders. Some wholesalers work with large chain stores and only accept large quantity orders. They sit and wait for orders and don't pay you until the books are sold.

Distributors buy books at a discount and sell them to retail stores. But unlike wholesalers, they actively market their stock of books by producing catalogues and sending a sales team out to retail stores to promote their books and make sales. But again, they won't pay you until the books are sold.

Jobbers aren't as commonly used as the wholesalers and distributors. They will store books and ship them as directed, but they don't buy any books themselves. They are simply a service provider to the publisher.

Most distributors want an exclusive deal with a publisher and can be picky as to who they work with. They also only deal with certain types of books, for instance, there are medical book distributors, educational book distributors and even Mind, Body & Spirit book distributors.

Wholesalers, on the other hand, don't mind who they deal with or who else a publisher deals with. They will also carry any type of book because they deal with so many different types of bookstores. So although they'll stock your book (for a fee) you'll still have to do all the marketing yourself.

But both distributors and wholesalers take care of all the paperwork including invoices, returns and payments as well as all the packing and shipping of your book.

Contacting a Book Distributor

Choosing a book distributor is one of the most important steps in publishing a printed book, so choose your company carefully, read every page of their website, consider every term in their contract and don't settle for a company that is going to offer less than you want.

When contacting a book distributor, keep your approach as professional as possible.

Only contact those that are interested in your genre. The best way to contact them, unless they stipulate otherwise, is by telephone. If they are interested, ask them to email submission guidelines to you. If they don't seem interested in working with you, ask if they know another distributor who would.

If you prefer to contact them in writing, explain to them your target audience, why you, as an author, were the best person to write the book, what makes the book unique, any previous sales records (from this or another book) plus your other writing successes.

It's also best to include a printed copy of your book so that they know the weight and size for packing and shipping purposes.

Territorial Rights

When books are published they are always published with what are called territorial rights.

Territorial rights used to be very important and books were never published without them.

These days, with so many books and eBooks being bought and sold online from one country to another, territorial rights are no longer as important.

It used to be that when a publishing company published a book, they would attach territorial rights to the book so that it could only be sold in the country in which it was published.

The reason for this was because in order to sell a book overseas, it was cheaper and easier to allow another publishing company to do it. For instance if a book was published in the USA, the publisher would assign territorial rights for the USA.

If they then wanted to sell the book in the UK, they would contract a UK publisher to publish the book and would assign UK territorial rights, which meant that the UK publisher could only sell the book in the UK. They would also do the same with other publishers in other countries, only allowing each one to sell the book in their own country (and in their own language) so that they didn't encroach on each other's customers.

But now with so many self-published authors and online book stores, books are regularly published in just one country and sold all over the world.

POD Publishing

Thanks to the internet and digital printing, POD (Print On Demand) publishing is now one of the most economical ways for an author to publish their book in printed format.

Books published using POD are kept electronically on file and are only printed when ordered, and shipped anywhere in the world.

This completely eliminates the need for storing or warehousing thousands of books which dramatically reduces the cost of publishing. Instead, copies of your book can be printed only when ordered and shipped anywhere you want.

POD also means that it's easier to keep titles "in print". Publishers used to only keep books in print if they were selling well. As soon as there was a slump in sales publishers would stop doing reprints and once all the stock was sold the book was listed as out of print. For some authors this could mean seeing book sales for only a few years, or worse, a few months.

But POD means that books can be kept "in print" for years. In fact traditional publishers are making available through POD, titles that they haven't sold for decades, so more and more books are coming back into print.

But you have to be careful of companies that claim to be POD publishing companies but are not.

These companies advertise themselves as offering POD for self-publishers, but when you read further, what they're offering is small print runs of only 50 or 100 books. But any printing company can do short print runs of books. And it isn't really Printing on Demand if no one except the printing company is demanding that the books be printed.

True POD means printing books only when they've been ordered by a customer or retailer.

Self-publishing companies usually allow you to sell print (POD) and eBook versions of your books. Some also allow you to publish audio books too.

Chapter 5.

eBook Publishing

eBook publishing is great because it's fast, easy and leaves you in control of your book and all your book sales.

eBooks are an electronic version of a book that can only be bought as an instantly downloadable document over the internet and the reader needs a computer or a palm-held electronic device to be able to access the book.

The advantage for the reader is that an eBook can be downloaded instantly and so there is no waiting to receive it.

From the publisher's point of view, the advantages are that there's no printing costs involved with producing an eBook so they are easier, cheaper and faster to produce.

There are many different ways you can format and sell your eBook, but we'll just look at a few ways that are cheap (or free), quick and easy.

What Are the Different Types of eBooks?

eBooks come in different formats for different reading devices.

The four most popular formats are:

PDF (Portable Document Format)

This is used for reading on a computer screen. It is one of the oldest types of eBook format and even today it is still the most popular and the most used.

.epub

This format is for reading on most eReading devices including Apple's iPhone and iPad. And Amazon/Kindle.

.mobi

This is the format that Amazon used to use because their eBooks were provided by a company called MobiPocket. However, Amazon bought MobiPocket and shifted all their eBooks to their own format. In 2022 they then ceased using .mobi because their updated software could no longer support it so they shifted to .epub.

.azw

This is Amazon's own eBook format which is based on MobiPocket but comes with its own digital rights management software.

Digital Right Management (DRM)

When setting up eBooks to sell through other online eBook retailers, most will ask if you want to apply DRM to your eBooks while a few will insist that you do.

Digital Right Management, put simply, is a downloading restriction that is applied to eBooks. Because of worries about piracy issues when eBooks first became available, it seemed like a good idea for publishers and authors to apply DRM restrictions so that customers couldn't share eBooks illegally.

But doing this created the same type of problems that happened when recording companies and gaming companies tried to apply DRM to CDs to stop illegal copying.

When Sony first tried to install DRM on its music CDs, the hidden files that controlled the amount of downloads a customer could do of their music, allowed viruses to conceal themselves in the hidden DRM files and corrupt computer hard drives. This led to Sony having to recall millions of discs that had the DRM software installed. Now most major recording companies have stopped using DRM.

In 2008 Electronic Arts (EA) released their much-anticipated game 'Spore' with a very difficult to remove DRM system installed. This system limited downloads to only three. Eventually, after several lawsuits, EA loosened up their DRM restrictions.

Another example of DRM gone bad was when Apple released the new model of their Mac Book laptop computers in 2008. These Mac Books were installed with High-Bandwidth Digital Content Protection (HDCP) which blocks any attempt of movies being played on analogue devices. This was to stop pirates using illegal copying software.

Unfortunately, it also meant that Mac Book users could not watch the movies they'd downloaded on external monitors connected to their computers.

But now DRM is no longer a problem since publishing companies brought out their own specific eReaders, like the Kobo eReader for all eBooks purchased from Kobo, and the Amazon Kindle eReader for all books bought from Amazon. These companies also provide a free eReader App that can be used on most devices including smart phones, tablets and computers.

So now the DRM mostly prevents eBooks from being used on other eReaders and eReading apps, which eliminates piracy.

These companies apply DRM to eBooks automatically so you know your eBooks are protected.

Before Ingram created their Ingram Sparks division, independent authors and small publishing companies had to deal directly with Lightning Source to get small print runs of their books or set them up as POD.

I used this company years ago, long before eBooks were ever a thing. It was always possible to produce 'How-To" books as downloadable PDF eBooks, but novels and other non-fiction books had to be printed and Lightning Source was one of the first companies to offer this service to authors directly.

But once Ingram introduced their Ingram Sparks Service, there was no need to deal directly with the printing company anymore because Ingram Sparks would not only print books, but make them available to over 40,000 book stores, including Amazon.

Ingram have a huge catalogue that they send daily to all bookstores, so it doesn't take long for your book to be available for sale all over the world.

Using POD and eBook companies like Amazon, Draft2Digital and Ingram Sparks, removes the problem of distribution for all self publishing authors.

Of course, there are other self publishing companies, but these 3 are the biggest.

Chapter 7.

Libraries and Legals

Libraries

Libraries are a much larger market than you might think because if only half of them bought just one copy of your book, it can add up to thousands of book sales.

For instance, there are over 115,000 libraries in the USA alone and over 14,000 libraries in Australia (at time of writing), not to mention Europe, South Africa, New Zealand...the list goes on.

As well as public libraries there are several other types such as specialist libraries (i.e. law, health, parliamentary), technical libraries, university libraries, high school libraries and primary school libraries.

Most libraries use Library Wholesale Companies or Library Supply Companies as they're sometimes known, who will buy your books in bulk, at a discount, and sell it on to the libraries for a profit.

It can save you a lot of time and money if you market to library wholesale companies who will then go out and promote your book to all available libraries.

Below is a list of a few Library Wholesale Companies:

https://www.follett.com/ (USA)

Provides books to school libraries.

http://www.brodart.com/ (USA)

Provides books to public libraries and schools.

https://blackwells.co.uk (UK)

Provides books to academic, research and public libraries.

https://www.bennett.com.au/ (Aus)

Australia's leading library supplier.

http://www.peterpal.com.au (Aus)

This library supplier is a privately owned Australian company.

Libraries are only interested in quality books that can withstand much handling. So when approaching libraries direct or through a library wholesaler, make sure you mention the good quality of your product.

Legal Deposit Copies of Your Book

In most countries at least one copy of your book must be given to the national library. This is called a Legal Deposit Copy. Other copies may be required by other state libraries. ISBN agencies can tell you where to send Legal Deposit Copies of your book.

For information about legal deposits in the USA, UK, New Zealand and Australia, try the following websites:

Library of Congress
https://www.loc.gov

The British Library
https://www.bl.uk

The National Library of New Zealand

https://natlib.govt.nz

The National Library of Australia

https://www.nla.gov.au

Obtaining PLR Payments For Your Book

Also apply to your national library for Public Lending Rights (PLR). This is money paid to authors every time their book is borrowed from a library or a yearly payment for each copy of a book that's stocked in a library.

PLR payments are only available in the author's own country and not all countries pay PLR. Surprisingly, the USA is a country that does not.

To find out your PLR rights in your country, go to

https://plrinternational.com

Extra note: If you're an author in the UK, you can also apply for PLR in Germany, Austria and The Netherlands by registering with the Authors' Licensing and Collecting Society (ALCS).

To apply for these extra PLR payments, go to

https://alcs.co.uk

If you are a writer in any country, you can also register for payments for photocopying royalties for any of your work that's published in a UK journal or magazine (print only). Find out more about these payments at https://alcs.co.uk

Libraries use a huge computer network to catalogue and control their huge stocks of books. So once your book is listed in one library, it will quickly become known to others in the district through the computer network system.

So don't overlook libraries when it comes to earning money. With the possibility of selling thousands of copies of your books plus PLR payments it can all add up to a substantial income.

US Tax Laws

Now I know that talking about tax is boring. I also know that talking about law is boring. And talking about tax law is even more boring. But this section needs to be included, especially for anyone, like me, who deals with companies in the US yet lives in another country.

Obviously if you live in the same country as the company you are doing business with, then you'll probably already understand your own tax laws.

But it can get very complicated when dealing with US companies from overseas.

Now first you have to understand that I am no tax expert and I'm only giving you advice here and now to try and make things as simple to understand as possible.

So don't take anything you read here as legal advice. Always ALWAYS seek advice from a tax expert first before you do anything.

But to help you understand the complicated maze of US tax laws, I'll give you a somewhat brief "heads up."

With US websites, you first of all need to obtain a US Tax ID number. This is easy to do if you live in the US and have a Social Security number. But if you don't, then you need to obtain an ITIN.

An ITIN, or Individual Taxpayer Identification Number, is a tax processing number only available for certain nonresident and resident aliens, their spouses, and dependents who cannot get a Social Security Number (SSN). It is a 9-digit number, beginning with the number "9".

To obtain an ITIN you need to fill out form W-7 and mail it along with certain personal identifying documents. If you reside in certain countries that abide by the Hague Convention, then certified copies of documents, instead of the originals can be mailed instead. You can find complete information about this at https://www.irs.gov, under "forms and Instructions"

If you do not reside within the US, the IRS will withhold 30% of your earnings.

Many countries have tax treaties with the US and if you reside in one of these countries you can claim full or partial exemption from tax withholding.

Some of the current withholding rates are

Canada - 0%

Australia - 5%

New Zealand - 10%

Germany - 0%.

To see more countries with tax treaties see pages 36 and 37 of https://www.irs.gov/pub/irs-pdf/p901.pdf.

Once you have your ITIN, fill out a form W-8BEN and send it to the company responsible for paying you your income from the US. On this form you need to fill out your ITIN, your address and country where you reside, the amount of tax exemption you are claiming and why you believe you are entitled to it.

Alternatively, you can telephone the IRS in the US direct and do everything over the phone in minutes. This is what I did, and it made it so easy.

I hope this brief introduction to US tax laws and tax treaties has helped.

But as I said, I'm no tax expert and I cannot offer legal advice.

All this information can seem daunting at first but as you go through it all, it will all make more sense.

And once it's done, it's done.

Chapter 8.

Marketing

Marketing is the most important thing you can do for your book.

Why?

Because people won't buy your book if they don't know it's there and they don't know how good it is.

And not only do you need to market your book when it's first published, but even when you're making good sales you still need to go on marketing on a regular basis.

All successful companies know that the only type of effective marketing is on-going marketing. That's why even the already hugely successful companies like McDonalds, Nike and Coke-a-Cola keep on marketing year after year. They know the power of consistency when it comes to selling their products.

So this is what you have to do as well.

Marketing is everything when it comes to making sales.

The author, Matt Dunn, put it best when he said, "a good publicity push can be the difference between the bestseller list and the bargain bins."

All authors, whether self published or trade published, have to promote their own work.

To market correctly, you must be sure of who your target audience is, and it can be more than one.

For instance, if you've written a childrens' book, you may think that your audience is children. But you may need to target your marketing at library supply companies, school librarians, schoolteachers, parents and also grandparents.

Also don't forget to get in touch with any appropriate website owners. Don't ask them to buy your book, but to promote it on their website via an online bookstore like Amazon who offer commissions for affiliate sales. Offer them a free digital copy.

Book Reviews

Getting a good review of your book can give a huge boost to your book sales.

Many readers are happy to put free book reviews online on websites like Amazon. But for these reviews to be effective, people have to be actively looking for your book, or one like it, in the first place.

One option is to search online for book reviewers to see if they'd be interested in your book.

Usually, these reviewers have a preference for what types of books they read and review.

These reviewers will have a list of email subscribers who they email their reviews to as well as posting it in their website.

If you send a printed copy of your book to a reviewer, they are not obliged to return it. It's theirs to keep.

Whether you send them a printed copy or a digital copy, make sure it's stamped as a 'review copy' to stop them selling it. If it's a digital copy, include their email address in it so it can't be shared and include a watermark that says, 'review copy only.'

Keep a list of what you send, who you sent it to, and the date you sent it.

They should send you a copy of their review. If they don't, and it's been several weeks, follow up with them to see what's happening.

There are also book review sites that have thousands of members who read and review books. The biggest and most popular one is Goodreads. They have millions of reviewers and it's free to join and suggest your book for review.

There are also websites that recommend books to their visitors and their email list. This type of service isn't free, but it can produce hundreds of sales. One of the most in-demand sites like this is BookBub, and there are plenty of others.

Your Own Website

This is a good place to market your book, and it provides you with a place to send all your prospective readers, and once they visit your site you can go on marketing to them.

What to Put on Your Website

Your website can be anything you want. It can be as simple as one sales page with a "buy it now" link at the bottom or as complicated as a multipage site full of hundreds of pages of information.

Some authors just have a website about themselves as an author. They regularly update the site about the book they're currently working on and even ask readers to help with research.

Many of these authors only write one book a year, but having a website and regular communication with their readers ensures that for every book they publish, they have a hungry audience waiting to buy it.

You can start up your own author's website or have a themed site. For instance, if you write historical fiction, you could have a website full of information about the period in history you are writing about.

Likewise, if you're a horror author you can have a dark website full of everything horror-like.

And if your books are non-fiction then you'll find plenty of information to fill your website.

Of course, your website could be a simple blog. Blogging software is easy to use and once it's set up all you have to do is write your blog posts and hit "publish."

Look for a web hosting company that offers a good domain name and hosting package. Nearly all hosting companies also offer one-click blog set up too. And if you need help they usually have plenty of instructions and can even offer a set-up service to do it all for you.

It's also extremely wise to sign up with an email service so that people can sign up to receive regular emails from you.

You can even set up automatic emails so that every time you post something to your blog, it gets sent to your email list.

15 Ways to Market Your Book Online for Free

There's no doubt about it, the internet is the best place to market your book because its reach is truly global.

But to do it right you must make sure that your book is advertised on as many websites as possible.

But don't make the mistake of thinking that all your efforts have to be aimed at getting people to buy your book. That's not the intention of online marketing.

What you need to do is create interest in you and your book.

Your marketing should be aimed at getting people to visit your website. Once there, they can find out more about your work, contact you for an interview or join your regular email list (and you really need one of those).

It's a well-known fact that most people won't buy something the first time they see it. Instead the product needs to be put in front of them at least seven times before they'll buy.

And this is where online marketing can really help. With a website, a subscriber list and your book advertised all over the internet, you can't fail in getting it in front of potential buyers dozens of times over.

You just have to remember that EVERYTHING you do online is purely for marketing purposes, even if it doesn't seem like it.

And when readers see your book being advertised the first thing they'll think is "what's in it for me". So that is the question you must answer all the time.

Don't just tell them how great your book is (they just think you're biased anyway), say what's in it for them.

Will your book touch them emotionally? Scare them? Entertain them? Inform them? Also tell them what they'll be missing out on if they don't read your book.

Remember! People buy benefits, not products. So use your creative writing talents to really sell the benefits of reading your book.

If you've already written your sales page, then all of the benefits can be found there.

So now you need to get down to the process of marketing online.

And you need to start with the one essential thing that all authors must have:

1 Your Own Website

Now I know this has already been discussed before, but it's so important because if you don't have your own website, it's harder to market your book online.

You need a website that includes information about you, your book and a payment link to buy your book (or a link to an online bookstore where people can buy your book).

And your website needs to be your own so that you have complete control over it, and you can change it, add more pages or update it whenever you want AND no one can place inappropriate ads on your site, which sometimes happens with so-called "free" websites.

If you self-publish your book through a vanity publisher you may be tempted to just use their "Author's Page" that they give you instead of having your own website. But be very careful. I once read about an author who did this. He promoted his book really well and he had blog posts and reviews all over the internet advertising his book with a link to his "Author's Page".

But eventually he changed publisher because the quality of the printed books was not good.

Sadly all the marketing he'd already done was still directing interested readers to his old "Author's Page" and his unscrupulous publisher had replaced his book on that page with one by another author on a similar subject. Now all his previous marketing efforts were helping another author instead.

I've also read about authors who think that they don't need a website at all. They publish their book, get it listed on Amazon, and other online book stores and then whine and complain that they're not selling many books.

If you want to sell your book then you need to make it stand out from all the other books. And the only way to do this is with great marketing.

So you need a website where you can market your book. This is a place where you can let your creative genius run wild and really blow your own trumpet loud and long about how great your book is.

All your marketing across the internet can have a link back to your website to bring visitors in droves.

The content of your website depends on what your book is about. And remember that you can even use your own name as your website URL, such as johnsmith.com. That way if you're planning to write more than one book (and why the heck wouldn't you?), anyone who reads and enjoys one of your books can Google your name and find all your books at your website.

2 Email Marketing

Having a website is one thing but having your own list of loyal subscribers to your regular emails is the best thing.

One-shot marketing rarely works. As you already know, you have to expose potential readers to your book several times before they buy.

All advertisers know that repeat marketing works best. This is why you hear the same ads on the radio day after day.

TV ads are often run several times during one show. Why? Because they know that customers need to have a product put in front of them several times before they'll buy.

All successful advertisers follow this same principle of repeat marketing. And it works for online advertising too.

This is why having a loyal subscriber list for regular updates, or a newsletter really works. Your emails need to be sent out on a regular and frequent basis either weekly, fortnightly or monthly. And the content needs to be top quality.

This is how your subscribers will get to know you, trust you and will want to buy far more books from you than from an author they've never heard of.

There's a saying in marketing that it's impossible to create a desire in someone to want to buy your product, but you can tap into a desire that's already there and turn it into a sale.

And when people subscribe to your email list, they've already shown you their desire, so all you have to do is build it into a sale – or many sales – through regular correspondence.

I know of one author who writes romance novels, and she only writes and publishes one book a year. She runs a blog all about what she's working on, what she's up to in her private life, research she's been doing for her next book etc. She has a large subscriber list and emails them updates of her blog every month.

And because of this, whenever she publishes her next book, she has hundreds of loyal fans all dying to buy a copy as soon as it's available.

Now that's clever marketing.

3 Free Book Excerpt Sites

Posting free excerpts online is a great way to gain interest in your book because it leaves the reader wanting to learn more.

The ideal excerpt to use is the first three chapters of your book.

If you've written your book "hypnotically" the ending of every chapter (whether you write fiction or non-fiction) should end with a "hook" that leaves the reader eager to read the next chapter.

So when someone reads the first 3 chapters of your book online, they'll have been "hooked" 3 times and will be dying to read more. And as long as the excerpt ends with a link they can click to buy the book, you're almost guaranteed to make a sale.

The first and most obvious place to post an excerpt of your book is on your own website.

But don't stop there, make sure your excerpt is available to as many people as possible.

There are also many websites that publish book excerpts. Just do an online search and you'll easily find them.

If your book is listed on Amazon, allow the "look inside" feature so that readers can read an excerpt and even download it.

You just need to get people reading your book and hopefully they'll want to buy a copy so they can read more.

4 Article Marketing

There are many online article sites where you can sign up and submit articles for publication. It's a great place to write articles that are related to your book's topic.

Alternatively, you could publish an excerpt from your book, if it's allowed.

These sites also allow you to include a resource box at the end of your article where you can include a link to your sales page or directly to where your book can be bought online.

One great thing about using article directories like Medium or Wattpad, is that you can leave your articles and excerpts there for years and they will keep on working for you.

5 Blogs and Magazines for Book Excerpts

To get your book advertised in an online blog or in magazine newsletters you'll probably have to pay. But if you don't want to spend money on advertising you could use your book excerpt instead.

People who have blogs or newsletters or even magazines are always looking for something that could be of interest to their readers and if their readers are a target audience for your type of book then they may be interested in publishing your excerpt.

Your initial approach to them needs to be brief and it also needs to be personal so that they won't think you're spamming them. So always use the name of the person you're writing to in your email.

Hi (name of blogger/editor/publisher)

My name is   author of   and I was wondering if you'd like to run a free excerpt of my book in your (blog/newsletter/magazine).

I would be happy to send you an electronic copy of the whole book for your review. Please let me know if you're interested.

Don't be afraid of giving away an eBook copy of your book. People don't like to recommend a book they've never read.

If they respond positively, email the excerpt or if your book file is large, ask them if they want you to email it or upload it to your website so they can download it from there. No one likes to receive massive emails that take 10-20 minutes to download.

But first you need to find your targeted blogs, newsletters and magazines. So start using Google.

For instance, if you've written a book about guinea pigs search for each type of publication about guinea pigs like this:

"guinea pigs" website

"guinea pigs" blog

"guinea pigs" ezine

"guinea pigs" newsletter

"guinea pigs" magazine

Search through the top results for each type of publication and visit each website to make sure it's targeted. You can also find the name of the person you need to email.

If your book is fiction, search for publications that target your audience, for example, if you've written a horror book then you need to search for horror readers. So try a Google search for "horror readers website", etc. Don't forget to try other keywords too, for instance as well as horror, you could search "dark mystery" or "vampire" or "horror gore"

Once you start Googling and trying different keywords you should be able to find plenty of people and publications to offer your excerpt to.

And once you've finished, it's time to look at a more subtle way to market your book.

6 Posting to Forums and Social Media

Visiting forums and joining their discussions isn't to everyone's liking. Some people thrive on this kind of social interaction, but personally I don't. I find visiting forums too time consuming. I do visit forums and join in or start discussions whenever I need information and I've even made a few "friends" this way and made sales. So there is value in this type of subtle marketing, but it can suck up a lot of time to do it.

Social media sites like Twitter and Instagram can also be used for marketing, and because they're so common and so popular, I don't think I need to go into detail about how to use them, except to say don't try and make sales. Just provide useful, funny or interesting information that others want to share.

Whenever you Google a topic, some of the results are usually from a discussion on a forum.

Most forums let you read their threads for free.

So search for a few different keywords and key phrases and use what shows up in the results or simply use the word "forum" or "group" or "discussion group" in your search.

When you visit a forum it will quickly become obvious as to whether the members could be potential buyers of your book. And here's a real valuable piece of advice. Don't join any writer's forums. These people are writers looking to sell books, not readers looking to buy books. They are not your audience (unless you've written a book about writing).

Start by joining one or two forums. Use the introductory section to introduce yourself first if they have one.

In your signature box start with something simple like "Your name: Author of..................". If people are interested they will Google the title of your book and find it at your website or online bookstore. A simple signature like this won't look like marketing.

But as I've already said, posting to forums can be time consuming so don't visit more than once a day or once a week.

Eventually you can change your signature to include a link to your website or a link to your free excerpt.

You may even learn a thing or two from visiting forums, but make sure that you don't get too caught up in them. Some people spend all day every day posting to forums, but you have no need to be this active on them. Use what you learn as something to share on social media.

Just make sure that you post useful, relevant and keyword rich answers so that your posts will show up in future searches results.

And speaking of Google searches, you also need to make sure that your book ranks higher in Google search results than any other.

7 How to get Higher Listings on Google

Sometimes you may find that when you search your book's title on Google (or any other search engine), another book on the same topic shows up above yours in the search results.

You need to make sure that your book shows up highest on Google search results, not just for your book's title, but also for your book's topic.

The reason that other books are higher is because their keywords are more relevant.

So you need to change yours to make them more relevant than any other similar books.

To do this, search for your book's title. Chances are that other books will show up in the results too, probably on Amazon.com.

Visit the book's web page, even if it's on Amazon.com, read the book's description and any customer reviews. Make a note of all the relevant keywords and key phrases used.

Next take a look at the page's source code by clicking on "view" in your menu bar and then "source code".

Near the top of the source code you'll see the list of keywords and key phrases in the "meta tags". Make a note of any that are relevant to your book.

Do the same for every book that is listed in the search results.

If your book is available on Amazon.com, edit your book's description to include your newly acquired keywords. Do the same with your own website. Add more keywords to your book's page and add them to your meta tags in the source code.

You could also use Google's free keyword tool to find even more keywords.

Once you've finished you can then sit back and let Google work its magic of getting your book to the top of its search results, while you move on to your next type of marketing.

8 Marketing with Blog Comments

Online blogging has really taken off during the last few years. This is because blogs are easy to set up, need no technical or HTML knowledge and are more personal than a website and so bloggers find it easier to write posts because they can write in a more relaxed style.

Nearly all blogs allow comments, and this can be a great place to subtly market your book because it's less intrusive (if you do it correctly) and it provides a link back to your website.

To find a blog to leave a comment on, do a search on Google for your keywords along with the word blog. Search for your keywords one at a time.

For instance, to find blogs that have a suitable audience for this book, I first used the keyword "self publish blog" (without the quotation marks) and it brought back thousands of results for blogs about self publishing.

The thing that makes blogs such a fantastic marketing tool is that the people reading and commenting on them are a pre-existing audience who are already interested in what you have to sell.

Not only that, but blogs are updated all the time, sometimes on a daily basis, so you can keep coming back to find new posts over and over again.

Blog comments can be used for on-going marketing as new blogs appear and thousands more pages are posted. But you need to be extremely subtle (and clever) with your blog comments.

Some blogs won't let you comment unless you sign up to their blog first. This is just a way to reduce spam comments, so if you find a really useful blog, don't let the sign up put you off.

Other blogs will let you comment without a membership, but your comment may take a few days to appear because it needs to be moderated first.

Comment boxes can usually be found at the bottom of a blog post. They usually ask for your name, email address (which is not for publication), your website URL (which is linked to your name) and your comment. When leaving your comment remember that this is your time to shine.

Don't make your comment too long or people may not read it.

Start it with a good hook that also acknowledges that you've read the post and the other comments. It's even OK to start by saying "I have to disagree with..." because controversy always gets attention.

But whatever you put in your comment needs to grab attention AND be useful. You need to impart some really relevant and useful information.

It's even OK to quote from your book by saying "in my book (book title here) I talk about this in depth, and I advise people to...".

Just mentioning your book title once is enough for anyone interested to Google it to find out more.

Because commenting on blogs is ongoing marketing, you only need to leave one or two comments every day on different blogs to get hundreds of links to your website and get your book noticed in as many places as possible.

And if your comments are relevant, useful and well written, you'll position yourself as an expert in other people's minds.

Blog commenting is an easy way to market your book. But don't think that because it's so easy it doesn't work, it does.

I once left a comment on the Clickbank.com blog and they moved it to the home page of their main site where it flashed up over and over again along with comments from other people. And that REALLY helped me to promote my newest book at the time.

And that's not the first or only time that's happened. There have been other times when people have copied my comments to prominent pages on their website or used them as a testimonial if I've said something great about their book/product/website.

And that's what can happen if your comments are good.

9 Marketing Through News Sites

Newspapers are now providing almost all of their content online for free. While they won't freely provide everything in their current edition, they do archive everything on their websites and many of them may also have a blog too.

News sites often allow comments much the same as blogs do, or they allow comments on their blog. They'll probably have a Facebook page so be active on that in a helpful and informative way

And unless your book has only a local target audience, you can post comments to news sites all over the world.

It's also possible to email a "letter to the editor" directly from the website of most newspapers, so don't overlook this free marketing opportunity either.

If you don't know the names of your local / national newspapers, or to find more go to allyoucanread.com where you can find links to magazines and newspapers all over the world.

Once you find a newspaper's website, search for recent articles on the topic of your book.

If they allow comments leave a relevant and informative comment with your name and book title as your signature and proof of your authority on the subject.

Sign your comment with:

Your name

Author of *Your Book*

If the newspaper considers taking the article further, they may even contact you for an interview or for further comment.

If you find a really interesting article on your book's topic and the site doesn't allow comments, email the journalist who wrote it and give them your comment instead, along with your author signature and book title. Your email should be in the form of a letter rather than an online comment.

The journalist may even want to use you as a source of information in the future.

And if you do leave a comment on a news website, check back again in case someone has replied or has asked you a question.

After all, your name on a news site, and your authority as an author, puts you in expert status.

And leaving comments on news websites and their social media pages isn't the only way to pitch yourself as an expert to the media, as you'll see in the next section.

10 Become an Expert Source to Journalists

So far we've covered nine ways to market your book online for free.

And while this section is also about using the internet, it can also land you with free off-line marketing in newspapers, magazines or even on TV and radio.

And you do this by pitching yourself as an expert or an interview source to journalists.

Obviously if you're the author of a non-fiction book you're an expert on your book's topic. But you don't need to be a non-fiction writer to be considered an expert.

For instance if you've written a historical novel, then you have knowledge about the era you've written about. Likewise, if you've written a detective novel you may have certain forensic knowledge from research you had to do.

Or maybe your expertise doesn't come directly from your book. If you're a mother of 5 and you've written a book then you're an information source for work at home mums. Or if you wrote your book during a long convalescence then you know about coping with a long illness or terrible injury.

Whatever your book is about, you're an expert or interview source on something.

Journalists are always looking for stories or quotes for their next (or current) assignment, so put yourself forward professionally and in a friendly manner.

And if you do agree to be interviewed make sure that your book or your website will be mentioned in the article if the article isn't about your book. Don't be shy about insisting on this as a return favour for the time you've given them. Journalists know that a good article will leave their readers wanting to know more, so your book title and/or website URL will help them.

To find journalists, you can search news sites like you did in the previous section.

Contact the writer of the article by Googling their name, if no contact details are available. Hopefully they'll have their own website or blog.

Send them an email explaining how you enjoyed their article, briefly explain your experience on the same topic, tell them you are an author and give them your book title and offer your assistance if they ever write an article on the same topic in the future. Make sure your email signature includes a link to your website.

Don't worry if you don't get a response. Most journalists, if interested, will file your email for later reference when needed. So it could be weeks, months or even years later before you ever hear from them.

But if your email was well written and you came across in an interesting and professional way, then you could be contacted for an interview sooner than you think.

And while you're warming your vocal cords for an interview with a journalist (which could also lead to radio and television interviews too), you could also prepare those same chords for a few online interviews.

11 Online Author Interviews

Marketing online can boost book sales immensely and help you to sell thousands of books. But doing an online interview will enable you to reach a whole new audience who may have otherwise not known about you or your book.

There's no doubt about it, if you can give a great audio interview, you can shine as an expert and influence many more people to buy your book.

People like to learn things by different means. Most like to use the written medium and learn by reading websites, emails, newsletters and free downloads.

But there are others who prefer to learn on the fly and so audio is the perfect way to reach them.

I regularly download PDF documents from the internet and receive several email newsletters that I devour for new information.

But when I'm busy doing other non-writing related things (such as cleaning, walking, driving, etc.) I listen to my MP3 player as I go. And I'm not listening to music. I'm listening to podcasts and interviews that I've downloaded from the internet.

And it's surprising how many people I've discovered this way.

For instance, several years ago I wanted to learn more about copywriting, so I searched the internet for free copywriting podcasts.

I came across a website of a copywriter called Ben Settle. I'd never heard of him before but he had several podcasts available of himself interviewing other copywriters.

So I downloaded them all and listened to them several times. I find that whenever I re-listen to an audio podcast, I learn something new every time, so I always listen to them more than once.

In one interview Ben was talking to a guy called Ray Edwards. Ray was a very highly paid copywriter, and he was so good at what he did that other copywriters hired him AND he charged up to $30,000 to write a sales letter.

So I looked him up online, was impressed with what I saw (and what I'd already heard) and signed up for his $600 web copywriting course.

Ben Settle then brought out a new book called "Cracker Jack Selling Secrets" and even though it was expensive (at $77 for one copy) and I had to wait 3 weeks for it to be shipped from the US to Australia, I bought it.

Why?

Because after listening to these two guys speak and realizing that they really knew what they were talking about, I wanted to learn more.

But no-one gives their really good information away for free, so I had to dig deep into my pockets to buy the expensive things they were selling.

Was I pleased with what I bought? Absolutely. Both Ben Settle and Ray Edwards are experts in their field of copywriting, though both in different ways.

But without free audio interviews being available, I would never have heard of either of them. And their products were enormously beneficial to me and have enabled me to improve my writing and earn much more money than what I spent on these two products.

My point here is that with a great audio interview you can not only reach a whole new audience of listeners who might never have known about you otherwise, but you can really come across as an expert in your chosen field and more people will want to buy your books.

But just remember that even though an interview done correctly can increase your book sales, an interview done incorrectly can not only hurt the sales of your current book, but also any other book you write in the future.

But don't let this put you off doing an online interview about a book you've written. The only way you can come across badly is if you don't know what you're talking about. And of course if you're being interviewed about a book you've already written then you will know what you're talking about.

And below are some tips to help your interview go really smoothly.

15 Tips for an Almost Flawless Online Audio Interview

To make the most of an interview you need to be prepared for everything that may come up. This means not only preparing for the answers you might give, but also for any distractions.

So here are 15 tips that will really help.

- Submit questions to your interviewer ahead of time and prepare really great answers for them.

- Know exactly how much time you have for the interview and arrange your answers to fit the time given.

- Practice your answers out loud before the interview to make sure you're communicating clearly.

- Don't try and oversell yourself. Your listeners want useful information, so provide what they're looking for. Only mention your book 2 or 3 times or only when invited to do so by your host.

- Be sure to give information and not sermons. Keep your readers "hooked" and willing to listen to your whole interview by summarising early about what they will learn. You could try saying something like "by the end of this interview everyone listening will have a better understanding of/be more confident in....".

- Smile as you talk. Even though no one can see you, smiling can be "heard" in your voice and make you sound more upbeat. It can also make you sound more interesting too.

- Disable call waiting. If your phone has call waiting activated, disable it.

- When you're being interviewed, give compliments whenever they're due. For instance if you're asked a really relevant question say, "that's a really good question and I'm sure many people want to know about that". This will help to draw your audience and keep them interested.

- Stand up. Your voice will be stronger and carry further if you stand while you're speaking.

- Have water handy. Your throat can get dry from talking for a long time, or through nerves. So have a glass of water handy throughout the interview.

- Get kids and pets out of the way. Children won't keep quiet just because you tell them to, and pets don't understand. So make sure there are no kids or pets around.

- Mistakes are OK. Don't let yourself be put off if you make a mistake. Listeners like to know that you're human too. So don't be nervous. Be impressive and if you slip up, just carry on.

- Get your listeners involved. Promises of things to come can really help your listeners feel like they are a part of the interview. So try things like "later I'll tell you the 3 most important things to remember, but first I want to share with you.....", and make a note so you don't forget.

- Plan a great conclusion. At the end of your interview give a good conclusion and a quick summary to remind your listeners of what you've said and what they've learnt. "This has been great. We've been able to take a look at.............and I hope your listeners have not only enjoyed this but now have enough information to be able to...".

Of course, if you want to do a video interview, some of this advice won't apply. But not everyone is comfortable using video, and I've never done it myself. And if someone approaches you and asks you to do an interview, get a list of the questions up front or offer some of your own.

Being prepared is one of the most important things.

Create Your Own Podcasts

A really good alternative to doing online interviews on other websites is to record and upload your own audio podcasts to your own website or to a podcast site.

To do this you'd need to have a script ready or have a list of points you want to cover. Using a script can make your recording word-perfect but can also make you come across as stilted and unnatural.

Having a list of points instead enables you to talk more freely and naturally but can cause you to ramble and get off topic.

But whichever way you choose to do it, creating downloadable podcasts is a great way to market your book AND open yourself up to a whole new audience.

If you need help to record and edit audio recordings you can download the free recording software from http://www.audacity.sorceforge.net. This is a free open-source software for recording and editing sounds. It has easy editing (copy, paste, delete etc.) and you can even edit out background noises and hissing sounds. And it's suitable for use with Mac, Windows and Linux. Your own computer may already have free software that you can use, like Garageband on a Mac

Alternatively, you can hire a professional to edit your podcasts.

12 Article Marketing

As previously discussed, article directories are great places to post your book excerpts. But don't forget they are also very useful for posting articles for marketing purposes.

If you've written a non-fiction book, then it's easy to think of articles you can write on your chosen subject. You can get ideas for your articles from your book itself by taking parts of a chapter and re-writing it into an article.

If your book is fiction, you can still use articles to market your book, but how you go about it will depend on your book's genre.

For instance, if your book is a historical romance, you can write articles about social etiquettes at that time or accepted dating norms. You can write about the need for chaperones or the ages that women were allowed to start dating.

Or if you've written a horror novel, you can write articles about the different types of horror (dark, atmospheric, gore fest) and mention more about yours in particular.

Or if your book is about vampires or aliens or werewolves, then there's plenty of history and myth you can write about.

At the end of your articles include a short and enticing blurb about your book and a link to your sales page.

But your articles need to be good so that other website owners and blog owners will want to re-publish them on their sites.

And if you can consistently write great articles, it's easy to build up a following of people eager to read more.

But before you write your first article, you need to be sure it's SEO ready. SEO stands for Search Engine Optimization and what this means is that your articles are easy for search engines to find and index correctly.

To do this you need to find out what people are searching for. So if you are going to write about vampires, you need to know exactly what kind of information people are searching for about vampires.

For instance, you might find that people are searching "do vampires prefer virgin's blood", so if that's a much-searched for query, then you could use that phrase as an article heading.

You can go use Google's free keyword tool to find the top 100 search terms of any word.

Any article you write should contain at least one key phrase and 2 or 3 keywords. Don't try and pack too many into one article or it will end up looking "keyword-stuffed".

The article heading is the most important part of an article and it's where you should include at least one keyword or a key phrase.

But most importantly, your heading must be intriguing enough to make people want to read your article.

For instance, instead of writing "Vampires Through History" as an uninteresting heading, try "Dark Secrets of Vampire Lore", (because people always want to know "secrets"), or "Seven Terrible Truths About Vampires" (even though there's no such thing as vampires so nothing about them can be "true").

But the point is that your headings must suggest that there is a lot of unknown or "secret" information in your article.

Make your article a minimum of 500 words but no longer than 1,000. When website owners are looking for articles to re-publish, they prefer longer articles to shorter articles. But if they're too long no one will read them.

Your articles need to have a beginning, a middle and an end and the best way to structure an article to achieve this is:

Say what you're going to say.

Say it.

Say what you've said.

Your article must also provide useful information for the reader. If they get to the end of your article and feel that they've learned nothing, then they'll feel cheated and won't be interested in buying your book.

Remember that readers will judge your book by the free information you provide, so the articles you provide for free MUST be good.

And using article marketing works best when it's done consistently.

So submitting your articles to the article directories every week, will produce much better results than submitting them less often and irregularly.

And every article you submit will carry on working for you for years to come.

13 How To Use Amazon.Com To Increase Your Book Sales

No other company has changed the way books are bought and sold as much as Amazon, and whether you publish directly with them or not, having your book listed on Amazon can do more for you than you think.

Did you know that:

Amazon sells over 100 million books a year.

They list your book in lots of different categories to get it in front of as many buyers as possible (something a bookstore won't normally do).

If your book makes a moderate number of sales, Amazon will do everything they can to increase your sales further including recommendations, wish lists, etc.

Listing your book with Amazon gives you free world-wide exposure.

There are Amazon stores in the US, the UK, Austria, Canada, Japan, China, France, Germany, Spain, and more.

This makes Amazon an easy place for buyers all over the world to find books, even obscure books that don't fit into a traditional marketing niche. Twenty five percent of Amazon's sales come from these types of books.

Buying books online is easier than searching through a bricks and mortar store and Amazon's free shipping offers and discounted prices make the online book-buying experience even more appealing for readers.

Amazon helps its customers find books they didn't know existed, rather than chasing block-buster best sellers like the small bookstores have to do to compete. And with free print and eBook publishing on their Kindle Direct Publishing (KDP) Platform it's now possible for authors to sell all their books on Amazon.

And on Amazon, book sales create even more book sales. The more you sell, the higher Amazon rates it in book searches. You can even suggest up to 10 categories and sub-categories that you think your book should be in.

One way to help online book sales at Amazon is to purchase your own book along with a best selling book in the same subject category or genre.

That way, when another customer looks at the other best-selling book, Amazon will try and entice them to spend more money by recommending yours and stating, "customers who bought this book (the best seller) also bought that book (your book)."

You don't need to go crazy buying your own book but try to purchase a copy along with a best-selling book once in a while.

Don't forget that as the author, you can also add your own information about your book to Amazon's website.

They also allow you to have an Author's Page where you can market yourself as an author and list all your other books too.

If you're just starting out with self-publishing, Amazon is one of the easiest ways to get started.

14 Social Media Marketing

Many writers use social media. In particular they use Instagram, Twitter (X), and Facebook. I've tried these ways of marketing, but I have to say that I'm not a fan. It seems like a lot of work and it way too easy to get caught scrolling through other people's pages, groups, and other suggestions (click-bait) that is thrown at you on these sites. But as I said, there are many writers who swear by social media marketing, but whether it helps sell books or not I have no idea.

There are some famous authors who regularly post on social media, but in most cases it seems they were already famous before they opened their accounts, and I have no idea if it helps them sell books or not. They don't seem to post about their books at all. They just post about their opinions on different subjects or repost things they find interesting.

Social media is supposed to be 'social' so it's unwise to blatantly market your books there.

But try it if you want to. I have the feeling that some people just seem to have a knack for using social media while others don't.

I, personally, don't like social media. It always seems like a waste of time, and despite posts being short, it takes an awful lot of time to create and upload them. Maybe I don't like social media because I'm not a social person in real life, and I find the falseness that so many people hide behind online, to be distasteful. There are people I personally know who are despicable in real life, yet their social media posts make them look like angels. Ugh!

And to keep up a popular presence on social media you also have to comment and 'like' what others post. That too seems so fake to me. And even if I make a positive comment, someone will always come back at me and say something negative. I often do a social media blackout and don't go on those sites for weeks at a time.

But if you're an online social butterfly, social media marketing will be right up your street.

15 The Big Mistake Some Writers Make

One of the biggest mistakes I see some new writers make is not being professional at all times.

The internet is a fickle friend. One minute you're a celebrated author, and the next, you make a mistake, and it quickly goes viral and ruins your reputation.

If you want to see what I mean, take a look at what happened to author, Jacqueline Howett. She asked a blogger to review one of her novels. But she didn't like the review he did (although I thought it was okay). She quickly became angry with him and posted offensive comments on his blog, and even stooped to using the 4-letter 'F' word a few times.

The result of it all was that the comments she made went viral immediately, she lost all credibility as a writer and had to withdraw her book.

You can see what happened at https://booksandpals.blogspot.com/2011/03/greek-seaman-jacqueline-howett.html. Her novel that started the whole episode, The Great Seaman, has its own Wikipedia page, all about her online tirade.

Another really good example of how viral unprofessionalism can go, was some customer support emails sent from a representative from Ocean Marketing called Paul Christoforo. The upshot of his lack of customer care skills and his almost abusive and threatening emails, was that the emails were posted online and went viral, causing him to not only lose his credibility but he also lost his job.

You can read all the emails at https://venturebeat.com/games/ocean-marketing-how-to-self-destruct-your-company-with-just-a-few-measly-emails/

If you're a published author, then you are a professional, so remember to always act like one. And don't think it's just the internet that can hurt you. Everywhere you go people have phones with cameras and video recorders and YouTube has made unwanted stars out of many people.

Chapter 9.

Quick start Self Publishing Guide

So now we're coming to the end of this guide about how to self publish your book and make it available worldwide.

So I thought it would be useful to give you a quick overview of what you need to do, and the best order (IMHO) to do it.

Feel free to change it up if you want to or even add steps if it suits, but these are the essential things.

1. A website. If you don't already have your own website or blog, get one. If you have one but it's not suitable for the types of book/s you want to publish, get another one. Make sure you have an online place where you can sell your books.

2. A sales page and blurb. You need to write your sales page for your website and the back cover blurb for your book. If your writing fiction, your sales page may simply be an extended version of your back cover blurb. I always think it's preferable to write these first because it can spark ideas to make your book even better. And you can always change it later.

3. ISBN. Your book needs an ISBN, and one for each version. Buy them upfront so that you can allocate them as you publish each book. If you're writing a series, the numbers can be consecutive if all bought at the same time.

4. Formatting your print book and eBook correctly. eBooks must have no page numbering and no page numbers in the TOC. Choose a font that is easy to read on screen but remember that readers can change it. Printed books, on the other hand must be formatted exactly as you want it, complete with page numbering.

5. Book Cover. Depending on how you're going to create a cover depends on how soon it should be done. If you're doing it yourself, you only need to choose (or create) a front cover image and design a front and back cover and a spine for your printed book, and/or a flat front cover for your eBook, If you're using a book cover designer give then your order as soon as you know how big your printed book will be so they know the correct dimensions, including the spine width.

6. Choose where to self publish. No doubt you already know how and where you want to self publish your book. But wherever you choose, it's usually a simple case of signing up for an account and making sure your book is formatted correctly to their specifications and uploading it once you've filled out the necessary information (book size, price, category, etc.). You'll also need to fill out your tax information if you're publishing through a company that is not in your own country.

7. 10-point marketing plan. Once your book is set up and ready to be published, you need to write out a 10-point plan of where and how you're going to market it. It usually takes a day or two before your book is available to buy so you can use that time to make a marketing plan and start writing all your marketing content. Also perfect your sales page and get it ready to add a link to where your book is now available. Don't forget to include library supply companies in your plan.

8. Write your next book. There is no better time to start writing your next book than when you're on a high from publishing the previous one. I'm assuming you want to write more books. Readers love to buy books from their favourite authors, so give them plenty to buy.

A Final Word

Self publishing really means freedom for writers and authors.

Why?

Because now you are free to go online and publish anything you want whether it's articles, stories, books, reports, songs, or anything else you care to write or create.

If you look around the internet you'll soon discover a whole plethora of people earning money from writing at home.

But as you see them all and notice how they're doing it, don't think you have to copy them. Whatever they're doing may suit them, but it may not suit you.

For instance, if you see someone earning a good living from their blog, don't think you have to become a full-time blogger too if you have no interest in blogging. Or if you see a fiction author selling millions of romance eBooks online, don't try and copy them if you don't want to be a fiction writer.

As the saying goes, Different Strokes For Different Folks.

You just have to figure out what kind of writing you like to do and go with that. Being a writer is a passion and if you're not passionate about your writing, you won't enjoy it, and ergo, it won't be good.

It can all be confusing when you first start out and you don't know what to do, but if the desire to write is there, you'll soon figure it out.

So What Should You Write and Publish?

Some people mistakenly think that they have nothing to write about. But that couldn't be further from the truth.

Everyone knows something, even if they don't know it.

If you're a parent, you know about bringing up children. If you're divorced, you know how hard that can be physically and mentally. If you work, you know about your job/career. If you like to knit, sew or garden, then you know about that. If you have pets, you know how to care for them.

So wherever your expertise lies in life, it's now really easy to set up a website around the subject of your knowledge. And when you've written enough articles and posted them to your website, then you probably have enough information there to gather it all up, expand it some more, and publish it as an eBook. And as you already know, you can format and publish and eBook in just one day.

And if you still feel stuck and you have more questions, it's easy to use Google to find more answers.

You can also sign up at my website ruthiswriting.com. This site contains hundreds of articles, products, courses, information and a whole lot more for writers and self publishers.

Self publishing is changing all the time, and it can change fast. Easy access to the internet seems to have put book publishing on speed.

More companies are opening, many are closing, and always there is change.

But one thing remains the same.

There is a hungry market out there for indie books. This has been proven by all the self published authors now becoming millionaires.

How Can You Start Making Money Self Publishing Right Now?

Only good writers make any amount of decent money from their writing.

Part of being a good writer means always writing for your readers and not for yourself. So don't just write and publish something just because you think you can make money from it.

People aren't stupid. They don't want to read crappy writing about things they're not interested in.

So write with your readers in mind and always publish your best work.

Self Publish Quickly, Affordably and Worldwide

Remember an eBook or print book can be published in just one day (or just one or two hours once you know what you're doing, and you have your systems in place).

And you can publish all your books for free with no upfront costs.

And selling your books worldwide is easy because the internet is global.

So now it's up to you.

I hope to see your books on the internet soon.

Wishing your all the best.

Ruth Barringham

https://ruthiswriting.com

* * * * *

End.

www.ingramcontent.com/pod-product-compliance
Lightning Source LLC
Chambersburg PA
CBHW072057290426
44110CB00014B/1726